S0-AYA-039

CONTENTS

MAJOR WESTWARD EXPANSION ROUTES

Fort Clatsop
Oregon Country from Britain 1846

Oregon City

Red River Basin from Britain 1818

Louisiana Purchase from France 1803

Promontory Summit

Sacramento

Omaha

St. Joseph
Independence

United States after the American Revolution 1783

The original Thirteen Colonies 1763

San Francisco

From Mexico after Mexican-American War 1848

St. Charles

Franklin

Santa Fe

Gadsden Purchase from Mexico 1853

Texas annexation from Mexico 1845

Florida acquisition from Spain 1819*

N
W   E
S

Major Trails of Exploration and Settlement:

Lewis and Clark return trip **1804-06**   **Santa Fe Trail 1821**   **Oregon Trail 1843**   **Pony Express 1860**   **Transcontinental Railroad 1869**

★ Trail begins
● Trail ends

* Officially ratified in 1821

 **Good Question!**

Who Were the American Pioneers?
AND OTHER QUESTIONS ABOUT . . .
Westward Expansion

WITHDRAWN

STERLING CHILDREN'S BOOKS
New York

STERLING CHILDREN'S BOOKS
New York

An Imprint of Sterling Publishing
387 Park Avenue South
New York, NY 10016

978-1-4027-9624-1 (hardcover)
978-1-4027-9047-8 (paperback)

Distributed in Canada by Sterling Publishing
c/o Canadian Manda Group, 165 Dufferin Street
Toronto, Ontario, Canada M6K 3H6
Distributed in the United Kingdom by GMC Distribution Services
Castle Place, 166 High Street, Lewes, East Sussex, England BN7 1XU
Distributed in Australia by Capricorn Link (Australia) Pty. Ltd.
P.O. Box 704, Windsor, NSW 2756, Australia

Design by Elizabeth Philips and Andrea Miller
Art by Robert Barrett

For information about custom editions, special sales, and premium and corporate purchases,
please contact Sterling Special Sales at 800-805-5489 or specialsales@sterlingpublishing.com.

Manufactured in China
Lot #:
2 4 6 8 10 9 7 5 3 1
10/13

www.sterlingpublishing.com/kids

Who were the American pioneers?

American pioneers were the brave individuals who risked everything to move west so they could find a better life. In the process, they helped build America.

When the Revolutionary War ended in 1783, North America was a vast wilderness. Only the section of land east of the Mississippi River belonged to the United States. Other foreign countries owned the rest. In 1803, President Thomas Jefferson bought eight hundred thousand square miles of land from France. The sale was called the Louisiana Purchase. It doubled the size of the United States, which now stretched from the Atlantic Ocean to the beginning of the Rocky Mountains.

Jefferson sent explorers Lewis and Clark three thousand miles into the northwestern part of the new territory. Accounts of their famous journey sparked the imaginations of people back east who wanted to see this new land.

Over the next fifty years, the United States again doubled its landmass by winning a war with Mexico and by signing treaties with Britain and Spain. What started as a trickle of adventurous pioneers steadily grew into a flood of settlers. They wanted to stretch the United States "from sea to shining sea." Some people even thought it was their religious duty. This feeling came to be known as Manifest Destiny.

The early pioneers first traveled west in search of a better life. The earliest ones sought furs. Then they sought gold. Most who came later sought good farmland. Some pushed west for lumber, some wanted vast tracts of land to graze their livestock, and some went west for the chance to start new businesses or churches. All had setbacks and sometimes terrible suffering. But in the end, the pioneers helped to create the America of today.

Who were the mountain men of the West?

Drawn by the quest for excitement and money, the fearless mountain men were the first to travel west and push across the Great Plains to reach the Rocky Mountains.

During the early 1800s, hats made from beaver skins were the height of fashion in Europe and the demand for the fur was high. Trappers and traders could make money selling beaver pelts. The mountain men traveled far into the West to find these skins. Many met Native Americans, who traded their animal pelts for metal goods such as pots, pans, and, later, guns.

While traveling through unknown territory, the mountain men found new river routes to western lands and new passes through the treacherous Rocky Mountains. They came back with exciting tales about the wilderness and blazed the way for settlers who would follow.

What was gold fever?

On January 24, 1848, a carpenter in Northern California found a chunk of yellow ore. It was gold! This discovery at Sutter's Mill started a frenzy known as gold fever across the country. People left everything behind for the chance to become rich.

Within a year, four thousand gold miners known as prospectors were working near the original gold strike. In 1849, more than ninety thousand people moved to California. By 1855, about three hundred thousand people had joined the gold rush. Most of the miners were Americans, while many others came from Europe, Latin America, and Asia.

Many of the prospectors who joined the gold rush were in such a hurry to get rich they did not prepare well for the wilderness. Many suffered or even died. Some people did get rich though, and others found different ways to prosper in the Golden West. Some became farmers and ranchers, while others set up businesses in new towns.

Miners pan for gold in California.

Pioneers left their overcrowded cities for a new life in the West.

Why did pioneer families risk it all to move west?

In the middle of the 1800s, millions of people immigrated to America from Europe, escaping hard times there. But the new arrivals created tension by competing with others for good hunting, farming lands, and jobs.

Many moved to the cities to work in factories, and soon the cities became overcrowded and dangerous. Life for factory workers, including children, was exhausting and dreary. And immigrants, especially Irish people, had to endure widespread prejudice.

Thousands of people decided to move to unknown lands beyond the Mississippi River rather than continue living in the East. They had heard that the untamed lands in the West were full of fish and game, and that the land was rich and fertile. Farmers and factory workers alike were drawn to the chance for a fresh start.

But the West was an immense place. Where would the new pioneers go? The decision was often based on the groups that had gone before them. Earlier settlers like German, Polish, and French people wrote to their relatives, describing the promise and wonders of the new lands. So, many new pioneers headed for communities settled by people with similar backgrounds.

Soon, many of the new regions shared different European customs. For example, large clusters of French people formed in Michigan, Missouri, and Louisiana. German people founded the first American-born church, called the United Brethren in Christ, and it attracted settlers to Indiana, Illinois, and Ohio.

Another good reason to travel west was the promise of free land. To encourage settlers, the U.S. government passed the Homestead Act that gave each pioneer 160 acres of land. The only requirement was that they live on the open space and farm it for a certain number of years. This promise drew millions of people into the West.

How did early pioneers travel west?

In the days before trains and highways, people traveled as much as possible by water. Often, a family would pack all it could onto a boat and go as far west as possible by river, then transfer to a wagon. The Missouri River took travelers in a northwest direction. The Red River and Arkansas River took people farther south.

When traveling on a river, most pioneers used flatboats, keelboats, or barges. These low-lying vessels were basically big rafts with low walls around the edges that could carry plenty of weight. Sheds or cabins were built on top of the decks to store cargo. These boats moved along with the currents. They could sometimes go upstream when pushed with poles or when strong men on the shore dragged them with ropes. Depending on their size, these boats could carry from one to three families. In the 1830s, steamships started replacing these hand-driven boats.

But river journeys brought all kinds of dangers. These low-lying boats often hit sandbars, rocks, and even each other. And sometimes they flooded and sank in storms. Steamboats could blow up, break down, or even catch fire.

When a pioneer family traveled over land, it often used a wagon. Wagons were outfitted with wooden hoops and covered with canvas to keep out the rain and dust. In the early years of the westward expansion, the routes to the West were nothing more than dirt trails across nearly empty plains. To encourage settlement, the government began building the National Road in 1811. Starting in Maryland, it became an entry point for travel to the West. By 1837, the road stretched all the way to Vandalia, Indiana. As thousands of people a year started moving westward, the early dirt trails soon became well-established routes. The best known and most used were the Oregon Trail to the great Northwest, the California Trail to Sacramento Valley, the Santa Fe Trail to the Southwest, and the Mormon Pioneer Trail to Utah.

Pioneers heading west along the Platte River hauled their wagons upon a barge.

What did the pioneers pack into their wagons?

Only essential items for the pioneer family's new life were packed within the 10-by-4-foot wagon space. These included seeds; farming and house-building tools; and household items, such as candles, sewing goods, food, and utensils. Each family brought a gun, and most had a Bible.

The classic Conestoga wagon was the wagon of choice for the long journey. Its big wooden wheels with spokes were covered with iron bands that could stand up to endless miles of rocks and ruts. The sloping cover protected things inside the wagon, which was pulled by horses, mules, or oxen. Horses and mules were faster but needed more care than oxen. Oxen traveled slowly but could live on a poor diet and were less likely to break down. Also, cows could keep up with the oxen's slower pace, so they could be brought along to provide milk on the journey.

When pioneers traveled west, they usually joined a wagon train led by experienced guides. The long line of white canvas-covered wagons looked like sailing ships moving across a sea of grassy plains. Sometimes there were long "traffic jams" at river crossings.

The journey took several months. Settlers needed to leave early enough in the year so they could cross the mountains or reach their destination before winter set in. If caught traveling during winter, pioneers could be stranded along a mountain trail without food. Danger was always near. Wagons could break down, or the work animals could die. Wagons could tip over, destroying everything a family had. Illnesses such as malaria and dysentery could kill travelers along the way. Pioneers were always mindful of wild animals and bandits who preyed on wagon trains. And there was always the threat of hostile encounters with Native Americans.

Conestoga wagons traveling west were called ships of the plains.

Native Americans spot a long line of settlers traveling over their tribal lands.

Why did Native Americans and pioneers fight?

Long before any Europeans came by boat, millions of Native Americans already lived in North America. Some Native American nations made their homes in permanent villages, while others were nomadic, moving freely over the vast plains. They followed herds of animals, such as the buffalo, which they used for food, shelter, and clothing.

Native Americans lived in close harmony with nature and saw the land and living things as holy. When the first settlers arrived, the native people met these strange-looking outsiders with great caution. They eventually traded furs and goods with them. But, as more and more white settlers arrived, the relationship between the two groups changed.

Most settlers did not understand the Native Americans' way of life. They believed their God was superior to the natural spirits worshipped by many of the Native American nations. The newcomers felt they would improve the land by taking it over.

Ownership of land was an idea that was foreign to the Native Americans. European settlers believed that people could own a specific piece of land. Native Americans did not. Instead, they believed that land was meant to be shared among clan members. All of these differences led to the great struggle between the two groups.

As pioneers poured into the West, the Native Americans realized the newcomers meant to stay and take over the lands. Hoping to scare off the newcomers, some clans began to attack the traveling pioneers. Sometimes they killed or kidnapped the settlers. Early settlers built forts, so they could live behind high walls while guards stood watch.

Eventually, the government signed treaties with the various clans that forced the native people to move far away from their homelands and live on lands they called reservations. As a result, many Native Americans suffered, traditions were lost, and their way of life would never be the same.

An 1875 log cabin built by a Mormon family in Utah.

A late nineteenth century sod house in Minnesota.

What did the pioneers use to build their first homes?

W hen a pioneer family found an ideal piece of land—one with rich soil, a ready water supply, and room to grow—the family built a house. The main building material came from the land itself. If forests or woods grew nearby, the family could build a log cabin. Big trees were chopped down, and logs were cut with notches at each end. The logs were then firmly set on top of each other to form walls. Using a mixture of mud and pine needles or straw gathered from the meadows, the children helped seal the cracks between the logs. Floors and roofs were made from pieces of lumber that were sawed from other logs.

These log cabins became the symbol of the American frontier. They were small, sometimes only 15 feet wide by 25 feet long. Furniture was built from the same wood used for the cabin. Heat usually came from a large fireplace that was also used for cooking.

If trees were scarce, pioneer families dug a home out of the banks of nearby hills. Sometimes they built a sod house out of 50-pound blocks of compact prairie soil that were cut out of the ground. When using the steel plows they had brought with them, the settlers could hear the tearing noise of the grass roots as they pulled the blocks from the earth.

The grass blocks were stacked root side up, so the roots could grow up into the blocks above them and make the walls stronger. Walls sloped out at the bottom to support the weight of the heavy soil. The roof was made from strips of sod and was a never-ending problem. Dirt, rain, bugs, and the occasional snake fell from the roof in a steady stream. If it got too wet, the roof collapsed. But the soddy, as it was called, was cool in the summer and warm in winter, even if the dirt floor was impossible to keep clean!

Every member of a pioneer family worked hard on the family's farm.

Was life hard for the pioneers?

Life for pioneer families was difficult—and dangerous. Everyone, including the children, worked from sunrise to sunset to make their farms successful. The crops and animals needed constant care. But a heavy workload was not the only hardship families endured.

Many difficulties were unpredictable. A swarm of insects, such as grasshoppers or locusts, could wipe out a year's crop within a few days. During times of drought, families could be forced to move if their precious creek or river water dried up. Terrifying prairie fires and blizzards could roar across the land. Extreme dust storms could bury crops.

In a land with few doctors and no hospitals, families could not cope with serious illnesses such as smallpox, cholera, and malaria. And for a settler living alone, the isolation was overwhelming.

Why were farm families so large?

As a familiar saying goes, "many hands make light work." For pioneer families, more children meant more help. Boys and girls gathered firewood in the forest or collected manure on the prairie for heating fuel. Children fed the various farm animals—sheep, pigs, goats, cows, chickens, and horses—and collected eggs from the chicken coop. They carried water from a river or creek. Sewing, cooking, and most cleaning were considered girls' work, while boys often stacked bales of hay.

The most important jobs were done in the farm fields. Children pulled weeds so they did not overtake the crops. When boys were old enough, they took their place in the fields beside their fathers, plowing and planting, building fences, and clearing the land. At harvest time, everybody worked to pick the ready crops. If the produce was not gathered quickly, it could rot. The working pace became a frantic mix of daily chores and harvesting.

Did pioneer children go to school?

Some pioneer children attended school, but usually for only three months a year—from December through February, during non-farming months. Teenage boys only went for half that time because they were still needed at home, even in the winter.

School began just after sunrise and lasted until early afternoon. To start the day, the schoolteacher would sometimes call, "Come to books!" Students rushed into a one-room schoolhouse and took their seats. Children ranged in age from five to sixteen years and were roughly grouped by age. Older students often helped the younger ones.

The subjects studied were called the three Rs—readin' (reading), 'riting (writing), and 'rithmetic (arithmetic). Students wrote with bits of chalk on small boards called slates. Some students made their own quill pens out of feathers and used boiled bark or berries for ink.

What did the pioneers do for fun?

Pioneers may have worked long and hard days, but they also tried to make time for some fun. This was especially true in the second half of the 1800s. Modern machinery and more farm labor allowed for additional leisure time. And people found ways to fill it.

The settlers usually lifted their spirits by playing musical instruments, such as harmonicas, fiddles, or banjos. Picnics and church socials brought neighbors together for food and friendship. Children had fun swimming in nearby rivers or ponds. At Fourth of July celebrations, people feasted, made noise, and listened to speeches. Families celebrated Christmas with small gifts and a feast. Some communities had a fair or harvest festival once the crops were in. As time passed, people also enjoyed attending horse races, baseball games, and circuses.

Children in Montana attend a one-room schoolhouse in the 1880s.

Many small businesses line the street of this bustling western town.

Who settled the frontier towns of the Wild West?

Following the earlier pioneers were those who wanted to start their own businesses. They poured into the frontier and planned to make their fortune selling goods and services. Together they created small towns across the West.

Businesses that were the most useful to the settlers came first. A general store carried many different products, from hammers to hammocks. A blacksmith made horseshoes, tools, and cooking ware. A shoemaker and a barrel maker, known as a cooper, could generally succeed in a town of any size, because farm families needed boots and barrels.

Soon, skilled professionals such as doctors, tailors, and carpenters followed. From barbers to undertakers, settlers went west with the same high hopes as the previous pioneers. Eventually banks were founded by the town's leading citizens. And a community was not considered civilized until it had a school and church.

Compared to eastern cities, the western towns were crude looking. Rows of wooden structures crammed along a dusty street became the heart of the town. The buildings caught fire easily and burned down quickly. Many towns were rebuilt more than once before brick buildings took the place of wood.

The stagecoach station was another important part of life in a western town. The large horse-drawn coaches carried visitors to the town and delivered mail and news from afar. Visitors and locals mixed at the saloon, where settlers could relax and play a friendly (and sometimes not-so-friendly) game of cards. Typical of the "Wild" West, a few ended up in another fixture of the western town—the jail. Sometimes the jail cell was just a barred closet in the sheriff's office!

How fast was the Pony Express?

At the start of 1860, mail was delivered by railroad, and short messages were delivered via telegraph. But these services went no farther west than St. Joseph, Missouri. It took twenty-four days to get a letter from Missouri to California by stagecoach. Three Missouri businessmen set out to speed up things. They started a mail-delivery route that would cover more than two thousand miles and shorten the delivery time to just ten days. They called it the Pony Express.

About eighty young riders were hired. They were all small and lightweight, so their ponies could run fast. Some 157 stations were established along the vast route. Riders covered about seventy-five miles a day and changed horses every five to twenty miles.

In April 1860, huge crowds gathered in St. Joseph and in Sacramento. Pony Express rider Johnny Fry set out from Missouri, and Harry Roff set out from California. When each rider reached the opposite city in ten days, the nation was thrilled.

This amazing performance came at a price. Just two weeks after the service started, a rider was killed when he crashed into a dead ox on the road. He was not the last to give his life. A number of station employees were killed by Native Americans. But despite all the danger, only one rider ever refused to make a trip, and only one satchel of mail was ever lost.

While riders were racing across the country, they could see crews along their route, stringing the telegraph wires that would mean the end of the Pony Express. When the telegraph was completed, messages took mere seconds to go coast to coast. The new mail service was out of business.

The Pony Express had lasted only 18 months. But the image of the lonely, brave horseman speeding alone under the western sky holds a special place in America's story.

A lone Pony Express rider races across open country to deliver the mail.

Who were the cowboys?

Open rangelands in the far West were perfect for raising cattle and sheep. Thousands of animals grazed on large tracts of land called ranches. Many of the big ranches were located in Texas, New Mexico, and other southwest territories.

At springtime, the ranchers hired dozens of cowboys for the annual roundup. Cowboys, and some cowgirls, were superb horse riders and rope handlers. It was their job to gather the tens of thousands of cattle that were spread over miles of open range and drive them to an enclosed stockyard. Sometimes it took them up to three months to get to their destination.

A cowboy's life on the open range was hard and dangerous. Cowboys worked many long hours a day on horseback. If startled by a loud noise, the cattle could stampede, running wildly in all directions. It was also risky business to cross a deep river while controlling thousands of cattle. Dangers, such as poisonous rattlesnakes, lurked on the ground. And being out under the open sky made the cowboys and cowgirls targets for lightening strikes.

After a day's work, the cowboys gathered around the campfire for their meals. They spent the evening singing songs and telling stories of the Old West. At night they slept outside under the starry skies.

Once the cattle were rounded up in a stockade, new calves were branded with the rancher's mark. If cattle from different ranches got mixed together, they had to be separated into groups. Eventually each group of cattle was driven to the nearest train depot and loaded onto cattle cars. The train then delivered them to eastern cities such as Chicago and Kansas City.

In time, the range was fenced off and the railroad tracks ran right through many of the big ranches. Then only a few people were needed to corral the cattle onto the train cars. The cowboy faded from the West, but his way of life lives on in books, songs, and movies.

A cowboy and his horse on a roundup in the 1880s.

The railroad train helped settlers travel westward.

How did railroads help America's westward expansion?

The railroad played a major role in the story of the West. During the 1830s, railroads started appearing near major eastern cities. Rail companies started laying tracks between cities, such as Baltimore, Maryland, to Washington, D.C., and Boston, Massachusetts, to Providence, Rhode Island. Two decades later, more than 9,000 miles of railroad existed in the United States.

Soon the railroads crisscrossed the land east of the Mississippi River. Pioneers could make the rail trip from anywhere along the eastern shore of the United States to the Mississippi River and start their hard journey to the West from that point.

Railroads were not just for transporting people. Farmers and ranchers started using the railroads to move their products to distant markets. Because travel was so efficient, the cost of moving food products dropped dramatically. America developed into a rich farming nation.

Through the 1862 Act, Congress called for a transcontinental railroad that would eventually stretch from the Atlantic to the Pacific. It would become one of the biggest construction projects of all time. The Union Pacific Railroad laid 1,087 miles of track westward from Omaha, Nebraska, and the Central Pacific Railroad built 690 miles of track eastward from Sacramento, California. The Central Pacific Railroad might have had fewer miles to build, but it had tough mountain terrain to cross. Thousands of Chinese and Irish immigrants labored fearlessly, and many died along the way. After seven years, a spike made of gold fastened the final length of track and united the two lines at Promontory Summit in the Utah Territory in 1869. The East was now connected to the West by the transcontinental railroad. Now pioneers had an even easier journey to get to the West—and many took advantage of it.

What was the last big push into the West?

With the transcontinental railroad complete, settlers continued moving west at an even faster pace. Whenever the government opened new sections of land for settlement, the pioneers quickly snatched them.

In 1889, the government announced that two million acres of land in Oklahoma were now available to settlers. A race—called a land rush—was held. On April 22, about 50,000 hopeful settlers gathered on the borders of Oklahoma, each ready to claim of piece of land.

When the starting cannon sounded at noon, people in wagons, on foot, and on horseback poured over the borders to claim the best parcels of land. The land rush was so swift and wild that by sunset the population of Guthrie, Oklahoma, soared to ten thousand.

Not everyone played fairly during the race. Some illegally snuck onto the vacant land before the race started and were labeled "sooners." Today, Oklahoma is known as the Sooner State.

By 1890, no large unpopulated areas of land remained in the United States. The nation was settled from coast to coast.

What do we owe the pioneers?

The pioneers helped build America. With determination, creativity, and good humor, they faced a wilderness and made it their home. In the process, they defined America's personality.

Today, there are still new frontiers to explore. We need only to look out into space, under the ocean, inside the human body, and within the tiny world of the atom. Americans can still learn from the example of the brave and hopeful pioneers.

Astronaut Buzz Aldrin is a modern-day pioneer who traveled to the moon in 1969.

WESTWARD EXPANSION TIMELINE

1783 SEPTEMBER 3 — The Revolutionary War ends. Thirteen states and other U.S. territories stretch from the Atlantic Ocean to the Mississippi River.

1803 APRIL 30 — President Thomas Jefferson acquires the Louisiana Purchase from France, doubling the size of the United States.

1804 MAY 14 — Lewis and Clark start to explore new territories in the Northwest.

1806 MARCH 29 — Jefferson authorizes construction of the National Road from Maryland to Illinois.

1830 JANUARY 7 — The Baltimore and Ohio Railroad opens its initial mile-and-a-half stretch of the first passenger rail line in the United States.

1845 DECEMBER 29 — America officially adds Texas as a state, leading to war with Mexico.

1846 JUNE 15 — United States signs a treaty with Great Britain and gains the Northwest Territory.

1848 JANUARY 24 — Gold is discovered at Sutter's Mill, in California. When word gets out, prospectors overrun California, starting a gold rush.

FEBRUARY 2 — Following the Mexican-American War, Mexico gives more southwestern land to the United States.

1860 APRIL 3 — The Pony Express carries the first mail between Sacramento, California, and St. Joseph, Missouri, in ten days.

1862 MAY 20 — The Homestead Act is signed by President Lincoln, granting 160 acres of free land to settlers.

1869 MAY 10 — The First Transcontinental Railroad is completed, connecting the Atlantic and Pacific coasts.

1889 APRIL 22 — Fifty thousand people join the Oklahoma land rush for a chance to get free land.

1894 OCTOBER 22 — The U.S. Census Bureau indicates no frontier line exists.

For bibliography and further reading visit: http://www.sterlingpublishing.com/kids/good-question